CW01522147

EUREKA DAY

An explosive new comedy by
JONATHAN SPECTOR

DPS | A BROADWAY LICENSING IMPRINT

DRAMATISTS PLAY SERVICE

For Molly, who cheers when the other team scores.

The European premiere of EUREKA DAY opened at The Old Vic (Matthew Warchus, Artistic Director), London, on September 6, 2022. This production was coproduced by The Old Vic and Sonia Friedman Productions. It was directed by Katy Rudd, the set and costume designs were by Rob Howell, the lighting design was by Jon Clark, the sound design was by Donato Wharton, the video design was by Andrzej Goulding, the composer was Jherek Bischoff, the casting was by Jim Carnahan, the voice coach was Charlie Hughes-D'Aeth, the dialect coach was Penny Dyer, the Baylis Assistant Director was Aaliyah McKay, the company stage manager was Greg Shimmin, the deputy stage manager was Alex Burke, the assistant stage manager was Louise Quartermain, the costume supervisor was Deborah Andrews, the prop supervisor was Emma Dymott for ROC Props, and the wigs, hair, and makeup supervisors were Campbell Young and Helen Keane for Campbell Young Associates. The cast was as follows:

SUZANNE .... Helen Hunt
MAY .... Kirsten Foster
DON .... Mark McKinney
ELI .... Ben Schnetzer
CARINA .... Susan Kelechi Watson
WINTER/UNDERSTUDY CARINA .... Rachel Handshaw
UNDERSTUDY ELI .... Alex Cartuson
UNDERSTUDY MAY .... Shin-Fei Chen
UNDERSTUDY SUZANNE .... Pippa Winslow
UNDERSTUDY DON .... John Vernon

The New York premiere of EUREKA DAY was produced by Colt Coeur (Adrienne Campbell-Holt, Founding Artistic Director; Amy Ashton, Managing Director) at Walkerspace in August 2019.

EUREKA DAY was originally commissioned and produced by Aurora Theatre Company (Tom Ross, Artistic Director; Julie Saltzman Kellner, Managing Director), Berkeley, California, in April 2018.

CHARACTERS

DON
Mid-fifties, White. Head of school. No kids.

SUZANNE
Early fifties, White. A parent.

CARINA
Early forties, Black or biracial Black/White. A parent.

MEIKO
Late thirties, biracial Japanese/White. A parent.

ELI
Late thirties, White. Jewish or half-Jewish. A parent.

WINTER*
Thirties to fifties, Person of Color. A parent. This is a walk-on role with no lines.

PLACE

The Eureka Day School, Berkeley, California.

SPACE

An elementary school library in an old building high up in the hills of Berkeley, California, designed by Julia Morgan or one of her imitators.

TIME

Fall 2017.

* Please see casting note at the back of this volume.

TEXT

Line breaks and punctuation are primarily a guide to thought, but also inform the rhythm. They may indicate a new thought, a self-correction, a clarification, a parenthetical, an added emphasis, or a search for the right word.

A "/" marks the point of interruption.

Words in [ ] are not spoken.

When a line is indented, it indicates a continuation of the previous line. When there is no indentation, it indicates a line break. The exception to this is towards the end of Scene 3, when there are three columns of text. Spacing does not allow indentation in this section, so use your own judgment as to when a line is a break or when it is continuous.

The one saith, "This is my son that liveth, and thy son is the dead," and the other saith, "Nay; but thy son is the dead, and my son is the living."

And the king said, "Bring me a sword." And they brought a sword before the king.

And the king said, "Divide the living child in two, and give half to the one, and half to the other."

—Kings 3:23

"This is an important vaccine from a public health standpoint," [Dr. Bob] writes of the hep B vaccine, "but it's not as critical from an individual point of view." In order for this to make sense, one must believe that individuals are not part of the public.

—Eula Biss, *On Immunity*

EUREKA DAY

ACT ONE

Scene 1

An elementary school library in an old building high up in the Berkeley hills, designed by Julia Morgan or one of her imitators. A view of Golden Gate or Bay Bridge (or possibly both) out the window.

The books are divided into three sections: Fiction, Non-Fiction, and Social Justice. Bordering the room is lettering and images from progressive educational materials, such as the alphabet book A Is for Activist.* *Posters adorn the walls: "Berkeley Stands United Against Hate," "We Are The Resistance," "We Acknowledge the Chochenyo-Speaking Ohlone People as the Indigenous Stewards of this Land."*

A large banner reads: "WELCOME TO YOUR 2017–2018 SCHOOL YEAR."

Don, Eli, Carina, Meiko, and Suzanne sit in adult-sized chairs around a square of child-sized tables that have been pushed together. A plate of half-eaten scones sits at the center. Throughout the scene, Meiko is knitting. As the new person, Carina is seated in the middle.

MEIKO
personally no
I don't find it offensive
the term *itself* is not offensive

---

* See note on Songs/Recordings, Images, or Other Production Design Elements at the back of this volume.

ELI
(Helpfully.)
it's descriptive

SUZANNE
I think she's saying
I'm not putting words in your mouth
she's saying it's not *offensive*
but when you contextualize it in that *way*

MEIKO
I find
the best way not to put words in someone's mouth is not to put
    words in their mouth

DON
okay okay

SUZANNE
sorry sorry

MEIKO
it's fine

what I meant was
that we'd want to make it absolutely clear that it's optional
that it's not
Either
Or

SUZANNE
right
and *also*

that the inclusion of the term on this list *at all* is
I think
inappropriate?
and that some people *may*

With Good Reason
find its inclusion offensive

ELI
no no yeah

I just wonder though
by leaving it off

is it possible some people would find its *absence* offensive?

DON
you're concerned
that it could be a sort of
negation
of people's experience?

ELI
right
if our Core Operating Principle here is that everyone should
Feel Seen
by this community

SUZANNE
there's no benefit in Feeling Seen if you're simultaneously being *Othered*

MEIKO
well
no yeah

    A little moment.

DON
Carina did you want to
do you want to
offer anything?

CARINA
oh I

I'm happy to defer
I don't know that I've really formed a strong [opinion]

DON
that's perfectly all right
even just your gut instinct is [welcomed]
this is an Open Room
we *welcome* your unique perspective

CARINA
okay
uhhhh
thank you

will you just
can you remind me what the dropdown menu currently says?

ELI
surrrrrrrrrre
(Pulling it up on his phone.)
okay it's
the list is alphabetical just FYI
African-American or Black
East Asian Heritage
European Heritage or White
First Nations comma Indigenous and Aboriginal comma Native
    American Heritage
Latinx or Chicanx Heritage
Middle Eastern or Arab comma West Asian Heritage
Multiracial
Pacific Islander or Native Hawaiian Heritage
South Asian Heritage
Southeast Asian Heritage
and

Other

> *A little beat.*

CARINA
that seems pretty [comprehensive]
doesn't it?
it strikes me as
comprehensive?

MEIKO
a lot of thought went into it

ELI
look
it's possible because of my cousin's kids
I may have some Deeper Learning around this issue than you all do?
so
I just think
why not err on the side of *more* inclusivity
right?

SUZANNE
so
the *reason* not to Eli would be

the term Transracial Adoptee is [not appropriate]

the fact that you are adopted does not *change* your / [race]

ELI
I don't think anyone's saying that

SUZANNE
it's just
my understanding of that term is
is that it's a way to think about our
Cultural Identity   ELI
                                                        suresuresure
and also to think about how it *impacts*
                                                        it's complicated
the way our racial identity is formulated
and created over time

13

CARINA
so that makes [sense]
that actually sounds right to me

I mean I can just / say as a [Black Woman]

ELI
oh oh oh
sorry to cut you off but I wonder

CARINA
no no no [go ahead]

I wonder if there's a better *frame*
for this conversation which is:
who is the dropdown menu for?

DON
for prospective parents

ELI
no no no okay

SUZANNE
maybe a way to think about
        it is
if you are pulled over by the
        police they don't

obviously

they don't *ask* you if you were
        adopted

sure

MEIKO
oh that's a good
that's a really a good [point]

but
also
there's the perception of our community as we're viewed from the
        outside
say a picture on the website or in a brochure
of course people are gonna make certain assumptions
because we live in a racist society that applies race as a primary lens

or

is this about how we Perceive Ourselves?
so it's more
From The Inside Out

DON
you're suggesting
the *starting point* is identity?

ELI
right right right   MEIKO *(Skeptical.)*
                                           mmmmmmmmm
CARINA
and isn't
I'm sorry tell me if I'm misunderstanding
isn't Suzanne's point
and I think I agree?
that we'd be conflating two very different / [kinds of things]

ELI
no no no
it's a question of *framing*

SUZANNE
I think that's right Carina thank you

DON
it sounds like there's a lot to unpack here

        A moment. They unpack.

ELI
okay here's another [way to think about it]
I frequently encounter situations where I'm filling out a form or
        something
and in the way it's laid out
there's a clear assumption embedded
that if you're a Straight Cis Couple
the mother is the Primary [parent]
and just

CARINA
I don't [know]
you know I don't remember
I don't believe so

ELI
where was that?

CARINA
it was uh
we did first grade at Cragmont Elementary
in North Berkeley?

ELI
ahh

SUZANNE
you schooled at home for kindergarten?

CARINA
no we did public school

in Maryland

MEIKO
(Surprised.)
oh
(I'm sorry you had to go through that.)
ohhh

CARINA
but you know Cragmont was actually a lovely [place]
and we could walk from our house but
it just wasn't a good fit for Victor   SUZANNE
                                                         (Empathically.)
                                                         mmmmmmm

and you know my friend Margot says

you can always spot a Eureka Day kid because
at soccer games
they're the ones who cheer when the *other* team scores

MEIKO
that's so true

CARINA
also we
my wife and I
we just really love this idea of him being in a place where there's
such a strong Social Justice Component?

DON
oh Carina
not sure if anyone mentioned
at these meetings
we make every effort to
wherever possible

to only use Gender Neutral Pronouns when referring to a student

CARINA
oh
okay great

ELI
it's a little awkward at first

CARINA
no I think that's wonderful

DON
we're not assuming you don't know *your* child's Personal Pronoun

SUZANNE
it's more about Instilling The Habit

CARINA
sure

DON
we've found that that
the culture we create here
in this room
as the Executive Committee
truly does trickle down

to the staff and the teachers and the parents

MEIKO
it does it really does

DON
and we also want to make sure we have a range of viewpoints
    represented
which is why we have this floating spot
did Suzanne explain this to you?

SUZANNE
more or less

DON
one position on the Executive Committee is always held for a new
    parent

ELI
so we don't get too
calcified in our thinking

CARINA
well thank you
I'm honored to uh

DON
thank *you*

I apologize I threw us completely off track

ELI
no no
it's fine Don
I
I feel *heard*

we can move forward

DON
beautiful

so
there's no need to alter the admissions form at this time?

      Meiko nods/shrugs.

Carina?

CARINA
oh sure yeah
I'll uh
(Raising a hand.)
I Move
that we don't change the dropdown menu on the admissions form

      They all look at Carina strangely.

DON
I'm so sorry I really should have explained
we don't operate like some other [boards]
we don't take Board Votes

CARINA
oh

SUZANNE
we only make decisions By Consensus

CARINA
got it

those scones were *amazing*
where are they from?

> *Eli starts to clear the chairs. Don helps him. Meiko checks*
> *her phone, reads email, sends a text.*

SUZANNE
(To Carina.)
oh I *must* take you
it's actually an incredible story
the woman who runs the place
she was a very
she was this High Level Theoretical Physicist
you know quantum theory or whatever
got into a terrible car accident
and could just
could No Longer Do Math
there was some brain damage and
I don't know Other Trauma

CARINA
that's awful

SUZANNE
and then one day she was watching a cooking show or something
and that
whatever part of her brain was previously able to hold
you know
these incredibly large-scale equations

was now able to
instead
to grasp *baking*
in a similarly complex way

ELI
Don
why don't you take off
we'll clean up here

(As they're exiting.)
and so she just started coming up with the
Most Amazing Recipes

24

Suzanne and Carina are off.

DON
oh
are you sure?

ELI
absolutely

MEIKO
(Putting her phone away.)
beginning of the year

you must have a ton on your plate

DON
well if I'm being honest
I do have the Kilimanjaro of email mountains awaiting me

ELI
we should really hire you an email Sherpa

DON
that'd be nice

you know how to set the alarm?

ELI
of course

DON
okay well
thank you
Eli, Meiko
that's so kind

ELI
it's nothing

       Don exits.

Meiko rearranges the tables; Eli stacks the chairs and carries
them out. A moment.
He reenters.

can I ask you a question?

MEIKO
shoot

ELI
did you feel like I was talking too much tonight?

MEIKO
(Yes.)
no

ELI
really?

MEIKO
you were fine

ELI
'cause I was starting to feel very self-conscious about how *prevalent*
    my [voice was]

MEIKO
no it was [fine]

ELI
yeah?

MEIKO
(Flirty.)
though
I do like seeing you be put in your place

ELI
oh do you?

> *Eli pulls Meiko towards him.*
> *They kiss.*

so
Rebecca's in Pittsburgh tonight

MEIKO
who's with Tobias?

ELI
the babysitter

MEIKO
and won't the babysitter think it's strange if you bring some random
   woman home

ELI
she's very progressive
we met her at Burning Man

> *They kiss again.*
> *She breaks it.*

MEIKO
sorry
you know
I shouldn't
Olivia's
she's got a little fever

I mean my mom's with her
they're *fine*
but she
you know
I'm sure she'll be asking for Mommy

ELI
oh poor thing

Lights up on the library, empty.

Carina enters. Sees she's alone. Looks around. Checks her phone to make sure the location and time are right. Puts her phone away.

She turns and scans the bookshelf, pulls off a book. Sits in a child-sized chair and flips through it.

Suzanne enters. Carina turns and sees her.

CARINA
hi

SUZANNE
no one else is here?

> *Carina shakes her head.*

hmm

(Sees her holding the book.)
that's my book

CARINA
oh
sorry

SUZANNE
no no you're welcome to it
it's on Infinite-Term loan to the school
it was one of Walden's favorites

CARINA
yeah we
we loved it too

what grade is your uh [son]

Walden in?
I don't think I met / [him]

SUZANNE
oh no Walden is in uh
in college now
my oldest

CARINA
oh

SUZANNE
yeah when the
when we first got a building
not this building
we used to be in an old church
and there was a room designated as "library"
but we had no books and no money to buy books
so all of us
there were about fifteen families
we loaned all of our books
everything age appropriate
Tropic of Cancer, Our Bodies, Ourselves those I still have
but everything else
which was a little sad at first
being home with no books
but also such a great practice to teach our kids
you know *where does this object matter most?*
on a shelf in our house?
OR
in a place where someone else could Make Use?

CARINA
that's lovely

SUZANNE
even now

we buy a new book
read it at home
and as soon as we're done
we bring it to the school

pretty much this whole bookshelf was ours

CARINA
wow

SUZANNE
have you seen Don?

CARINA
no

I just got here
does this

does this happen a lot
these *emergency* [meetings]?

SUZANNE
never
almost never

CARINA
great

SUZANNE
very rarely

      A tiny and just barely awkward lull.

CARINA
hey thanks so much for Saturday
that was so lovely to get to meet / [all those people]

SUZANNE
of course
and it's not like a formal [thing]

but a lot of us are there every weekend
you're always welcome

CARINA
thank you

SUZANNE
and Victor is *such* a sweetheart

CARINA
yeah
he is
right?

I mean if you'd met him last year
he wouldn't have said two words to you
being here
he's really he's really   SUZANNE
                                                                      that's so great

coming out of his [shell]   Mmmmm

yeah *it is* [so great]
and it's not their fault
but his other school was really not set up
to accommodate his / [needs]

                                                                      sure
                                                                      you know there's a lot of
                                                                      of neurodiversity here

oh
                                                                      we really value it

actually he's not um
he's not on the spectrum
                                                                      ah

he's just
he's
he has low processing speeds?
in some areas
so he can understand everything but

33

and he's *so* smart
I mean that was the problem
because his teachers
they knew he needed specialized help
but he
he would still get straight As
because he was so smart that he could
    figure out workarounds so

                                    of course

and they said they couldn't
legally
they couldn't get him the special needs
    support unless he was failing

                                    oh my god

right?
which is insane to me but

                                    that's nightmarish

well I mean I'm sure it's great for lots of kids
but
honestly we probably should've taken him
    out of there a lot sooner

SUZANNE
well the important thing is
you've Found the Right Fit

CARINA
no right
I mean I still feel kinda weird about us being in a
you know
Private School

SUZANNE
oh

well I like to think of us as more of a
Community School

        Eli rushes in.

34

ELI
where's Don?

> *Suzanne shrugs.*

where are the chairs?

SUZANNE
?

> *Eli, with a mild sigh of exasperation, exits off to wherever the Adult Chairs are stored.*

I hope you're feeling empowered in these meetings
I know it can be intimidating
we can sometimes be very Forceful Advocates for our [perspectives]

CARINA
oh no no yeah

SUZANNE
it's a big priority of mine
all of ours but me especially
that there's a range of [viewpoints]
that we don't only hear from the voices of the
the Full-Pay Families

CARINA
right

(Realizing what Suzanne is saying.)
oh uh

SUZANNE
which is just to say
you're essential here
don't let yourself forget that

CARINA
um

okay
uhhhhh

> *Eli renters carrying a stack of five adult-sized chairs. He begins unstacking them.*

ELI
is this about the bathroom contractor?
'cause I told him we should use my guy

SUZANNE
this company came very highly recommend by one of our families
(To Carina.)
they use only locally sourced materials

ELI
so why is it taking three months?
what're they like
forging every nail by hand?

CARINA
is something wrong with the bathrooms?

SUZANNE
no no
we're in process
we're converting everything to All Gender

ELI
which you'd think would be
how hard is it to throw up some extra stalls?
but apparently they're like
they're building the Great Pyramids of Egypt in there

SUZANNE
you know Eli
the pyramids were built by enslaved people we think

ELI
(Not sure what she's talking about.)
uhhh
yeah I did know that

SUZANNE
well
so [you should maybe be more sensitive]

ELI
?

> *A moment. They wait.*
> *Don enters.*

DON
sorry sorry
thanks so much for rushing
I really appreciate it

SUZANNE
is everything [okay]?

DON
yeah yes
I know I know I'm sorry
I just
I thought it was better to

I didn't want to start a panic
so I wanted to
I wanted to tell you all first before this goes out

ELI
shouldn't we wait for Meiko?

SUZANNE
(To Eli.)
did she tell you she was coming?

ELI
oh
uh
I
wouldn't know

(Covering.)
Don, is she coming?

DON
I haven't heard back from her
she didn't say she wasn't

SUZANNE
well then
why don't you just go ahead and and and   DON
                                                  okay

and we'll just catch her up when she gets here

DON
great
uh

here
why don't I just read it to you?

> *He reads from a piece of paper.*

Dear Parent/Guardian:

This letter is to inform you that a child has been confirmed to have
    mumps who attended the Eureka Day School on October 26th.
    Mumps spreads both via direct contact and rapidly through
    the air. If your child has never had the disease or received the
    MMR vaccination, he or she is at risk.

Therefore, if your child has no documentation of immunity to
    mumps he or she will be excluded from school until such time
    as it is determined by the County Health Officer that there is
    no longer a risk of exposure. During this period, we request
    that your child remain quarantined at home.

A recommended vaccination schedule is attached. Although complications from mumps are rare, they can lead to sterility in males, deafness, brain damage, and death. If you have delayed or refused vaccinations for your child, please consider this event as a reminder of their importance and urgency.

Yours,
Charles A. Kilburn, MD
Alameda County Health Department

>*A beat.*

ELI
well
that's a little intense

SUZANNE
can I see it?

>*Don hands her the letter. She starts reading it.*

DON
I spoke to him on the phone
he's actually very nice
very helpful

I'm heading out to meet with him in just a [few minutes]
that's why I asked you all to
and *thank you* for coming so quickly

ELI
do we know who it is?

DON
I don't know
and even if I did I couldn't
legally I couldn't tell you

ELI
no of course
but it's just the *one* student?

ELI
totally totally
like we did the Delayed Schedule
you know we spaced them out
and we have some friends who were like *that's still WAY too many
vaccines*
and other people who were like *you should NOT have waited so long*

which basically meant we got the side-eye from everyone

SUZANNE
exactly
and we don't want anyone to feel pressured
or shamed

ELI
buuuuut

I think it's probably fine
like I think people will get it
I mean it's clearly signed by [the health department]
it's not like *Don* is writing this letter

SUZANNE
look

if we decide
if our stance is
you know
the school is going to be a resource to direct people to
to different kinds of information so they can make informed *decisions*
that would be one thing

but to just have this go out to everyone and say nothing?
it feels Very Irresponsible

I mean they receive this official-sounding letter

CARINA
but isn't it actually just like

An Official Letter?

SUZANNE
that's what I'm saying

DON
I certainly was not assuming we would say *nothing*
that's why I asked you all to [come in]

and I think you're right Suzanne
that we want to be
sensitive
about how we approach this
and wouldn't want to be perceived as *adjudicating* or

any more than we would for
religion or
political affiliation or
dietary preferences

but this is just a document we're passing on
there's no *judgment*

SUZANNE
well to me Don
what you've just said is a little like
it's like you're saying
We welcome all religions
Now here's your copy of the New Testament

DON
that's
a little uh [extreme]

is it?

ELI
huh
no no yeah
I can see that

'cause it's like
is this what you're saying Suzanne?
that even if it's a message that we conceptualize as Value Neutral
we have to try to be cognizant of the way it's going to be received
'cause it's really more about Individual Parents' Responsibilities /
    than it is about what we are

CARINA
I'm sorry to [interrupt]
but doesn't it seem like
I mean of course that makes sense

but shouldn't we be
right in this moment
just like focused on
you know
Getting The Message Out?

SUZANNE
I think that's right
I think
I'm sorry Eli
but I think she's right

because our responsibility in this room is not actually first
as Individual Parents
it's first
as Custodians of the School

CARINA
no exactly

SUZANNE
the question isn't
what are my Strongly Held Personal Views
it isn't
what do I think is right as a parent
it's

what do I think is best for our community?

right Carina?

CARINA
I mean
no yeah of course

SUZANNE
and it strikes me that right now
what matters most is
like you said
Getting The Message Out
that we are *one* community
a community of respect

and just to reiterate the principle of:
I may not agree with your Point of View
but I deeply respect your right to *hold* that Point of View

ELI
no yeah
that's what I was saying

DON
so maybe it's
in addition [to the letter]
maybe we say something along the lines of
I'm just spitballing here

that we are a school of *choice* and a community of *intention*
and we come from diverse backgrounds and perspectives
but that we are all in this together
and that
that it's our diversity which is the source of our strength

ELI
beautiful

SUZANNE
and then at the bottom we could include links to resources
and say
here is some of the broad array of viewpoints in our community

I could point people to some very good websites

DON
great great

does that
would that work for you Carina?

CARINA
um I'm not
I'm not

to be honest I'm not sure I'm a hundred percent comfortable with that

SUZANNE
oh?

well that's
that's fine

can you
are you able to *articulate* what it is that's
making you uncomfortable?

> *The tiniest of beats. Carina chooses to not read "articulate"*
> *as a microaggression.*

CARINA
it's just
if we're saying
here's what the health department says
and then
here's something that refutes that

isn't that
isn't that taking a position too

isn't our position then
don't listen to the health department?

SUZANNE
oh I don't think so

DON
okay so
what I'm hearing is that / there's a need to balance

ELI
oh oh oh!
sorry to [interrupt]

I'm just thinking
this is such a multifaceted [issue]
I don't know if the four of us can fully *encapsulate* [the scope]
and we're always talking about looking for opportunities to
to showcase
to put our Values Into Action
so maybe this is a great moment for a

Community Activated Conversation

DON
hmmm

CARINA
what's that?

ELI
it's a
it's a bit like a Town Hall
but more participatory

DON
it's a new initiative

SUZANNE
last year we had an Eighth Grade production of *Peter Pan*
which
I don't know what they were thinking

so as you can imagine
there were some
Very Strong Feelings

ELI
and aside from the extremely problematic portrayal of Native Peoples
there's actually a whole host of Colonialist Issues in terms of the content
that I for one had been completely blind to
so

DON
and the C.A.C. was really
it was a very thoughtful discussion and there were some great
        breakout sessions
and we ended up
we came to
what I thought was a very [good agreement]
we set the production in Outer Space
and that really solved [the problem]
I think everybody ended up feeling really good about that

and ever since we've been
we've been looking for another moment to

SUZANNE
it's a wonderful idea Eli

ELI
thank you

DON
it could be a pretty amazing opportunity I think
to demonstrate for the students

to see how we can come together as a community
and exchange ideas around a difficult issue

SUZANNE
and if we did that
I would be willing to
would this work for you Carina?

we allow the letter to go out As Is
and
we let everyone know that before they rush into anything that
as soon as possible
ideally tomorrow
we'll be having a Community Activated Conversation
so that we can really
delve into

CARINA
yeah no that's
great
that sounds great

ELI
perfect

DON
you know it's like Sylvia Culman
she was the first board president before Suzanne
she used to always say
if consensus was easy, everyone would do it

SUZANNE
it's so true

> *A tiny moment, in which they bask in their consensus.*
> *Meiko bursts in.*

MEIKO
sorry sorry sorry

ucchh
I completely could not get out of the house

I thought Olivia was all better but
her fever came back
and now her face is all swollen

I think maybe she's allergic to gluten?

sorry sorry please continue
what'd I miss?

> *Lights.*

Scene 3

> *The library. Suzanne, Meiko, Don, and Carina sit in a semi-circle of five chairs.*
>
> *A laptop sits open in front of Don. Eli sits next to the laptop, futzing with it. A camera on a tripod is set up in front of the group and connected to the laptop.*
>
> *Projected we see the Eureka Day livestream page.*
>
> *All of them are in sight of the camera, but only Don can comfortably read the text on the screen. The others have to make some effort to lean over him to see it.*

DON
(Leaning forward into the mic.)
thanks so much for your patience everyone
we're gonna be ready to go in just a minute

ELI
they can see you but they can't hear you

DON
ah

ELI
yet

DON
got it

> *Don tries to communicate wordlessly to "hang on just a second."*
> *Eli futzes.*
> *After a moment:*

ELI
(To the camera.)
sorry about the feed dropping everyone
we have Achieved Liftoff

DON
all right

so

why don't we go ahead and get started?

> *The livestream conversation proceeds here. Footnotes indicate*
> *when the comment appears. Every comment is accompanied*
> *by a notification sound.*

Just first of all
I want to say how much I appreciate all of you taking the time to be here
um
virtually[1]

> *Don reacts to the notification sound, reads the screen.*

thank you Karen

> *He turns his attention back to the camera.*

now
I know for many of you[2]

> *Don looks at the screen again, sees it's just a "like" and decides*
> *to push forward and ignore the comments for the moment.*

1 **Karen Sapp.** We can hear you now Don.

2 **Leslie Kaufman.** [Thumbs-up emoji]

and for myself
it's been a Very Chaotic
and very frightening
couple of days

ELI
actually Don
it's better for the video if you just sit back in your chair naturally
the sound quality's fine I'm pretty sure

> *Don sits back.*

DON
right[3]

I wish we could be together here
physically
but we were informed by the health department that was Not Advisable
so[4]

just to do a little framing[5]
the way we're thinking about this is

a series of concentric circles
those of us here in this room are a tiny circle[6]

and we're going to be having a conversation about what's happening
    in our community[7]
and we'll try to answer your questions
and those of you watching and commenting on the livestream[8]
you're a larger circle that envelops
and informs us

---

3 **Bryan Serulnak.** Any update on when school's reopening?

4 **Guita Lakani.** I think that's what they're about to tell us.

5 **Mikeala Morse-Turner.** Is Hallie not on the board anymore?

6 **Delia Perez.** They moved to Vancouver.

7 **Leslie Kaufman.** [Sad-face emoji]

8 **Myla Townes.** I'm pretty sure it was Montreal.

Also during this:
Eli gets a text. Reads it, replies quickly.
Meiko sees him do this. Gives him a quizzical look.
He looks up. Sees her look. Gives her a smile/shrug and puts
his phone away.
They both turn to the camera.

and then there's the even larger circle of the people in our community[9]
who are not able to participate right now in this conversation
and so it's[10]
all of our responsibility to to
Hold Stake for them
and bring their concerns and ideas into these circles as much as we can[11]

and also I want to say
as you're probably aware
there are a lot of eyes on us right now[12]
I know some of you have been contacted by the media
and
people are wondering how a community like ours is going to respond
    to this kind of uh[13]
adversity
so
I'd like to ask everyone to just be very
conscious
of our speech and to be aware[14]
that while this is a conversation *for* our community

---

9 **Delia Perez.** Actually we visited them in Vancouver over the summer.

10 **Delia Perez.** They're really happy there!

11 **Leslie Kaufman.** [Thumbs-up emoji]

12 **Taylor Aberra-Harris.** Is this a recording or is this live?

13 **Tyler Coppins.** It's live. Hence the term, "LIVESTREAM!"

14 **Arnold Filmore.** In fairness, you CAN watch recordings of old ones

we
each of us[15]
as individuals
are also representatives *of* that community[16]

so let's do our best to make sure we all keep our conversation
truthful
and helpful[17]
and supportive

is there anything you wanted to add Suzanne?

SUZANNE
oh
thanks Don
I'll just say
as you know
this community means so much to me[18]
and has been a part of my life for so long
and
I know there's a lot of anxiety right now[19]
and I'm just
I'm trying to
I'm keeping my heart open to all of you
and I know that you'll all do the same[20]

DON
also[21]

---

15 **Marla Nonner.** All four of us are watching!!!

16 **Tonya Wallace.** Samara and Tom aren't able to watch but they wanted me to say they wish they could.

17 **Svetlana Givental.** I can see the video but still can't hear. Can anyone else hear?

18 **Orson Mankel.** Svetlana, you might have it muted. Click the little speaker icon on bottom right.

19 **Svetlana Givental.** Thank you Orson!

20 **Dara Konrad.** Oh Suzanne!

21 **Leslie Kaufman.** [Thumbs-up emoji]

joining us virtually we have uh

on the livestream is Sarah Howell who's the parent of a fourth grader
and is a pediatrician

and is making herself available to answer any immediate um [medical
questions]

are you there Sarah?

> *Don looks at the comments. Everyone else leans in to see.*
> *A beat, then:*

[22]

okay

> *Don turns his gaze back to the camera.*
> *As does everyone else except Eli, who receives another text*
> *and gets involved in a text exchange, while still trying to give*
> *half his attention to the group conversation.*

so

what we know right now is

we are aware of fifteen students who have contracted mumps

but it might be

it's still early[23]

we're expecting ultimately the number may be much higher[24]

and I wonder Sarah would you

can you let everybody know the uh

the symptoms to look for?

> *Don reads the messages.*

MEIKO

I can also jump in here and say

Don I know you can't say anything but I'm allowed to[25]

I mean I can *out* myself, right?

so our family

---

22 **Sarah Howell.** Hi Everybody :)

23 **Pila Baum.** WHOA

24 **Sandy Washington.** Pretty sure Callie doesn't have mumps, just the regular flu.

25 **Sarah Howell.** symptoms include fever, headache, muscle aches, fatigue, loss of appetite, pain while chewing or swallowing, and swollen salivary glands.

Olivia had it, has it[26]
and I can say / for us there was

SUZANNE
oh Meiko
we're trying not to use the term "outed"[27]

MEIKO
(To Suzanne.)
hmmm?

SUZANNE
it's just a bit loaded
that term has a sort of historical association with shame[28]

maybe a more neutral [term]?

> *Mini-beat. Meiko masks her annoyance.*

MEIKO
sure

anyway um[29]
what was I [saying]?

oh so
Olivia had a fever
that kind of came and went annnnnd
her face got very swollen like uh[30]
like when you get your wisdom teeth [out]?

but she's really

---

26 **Sarah Howell.** If you think your child has any of these symptoms please contact your doctor IMMEDIATELY.

27 **Deborah Roth.** Is it okay to take Tylenol for fever?

28 **Sarah Howell.** Acetaminophen or ibuprofen is fine. Just not aspirin.

29 **Darla Campese.** I'd also suggest ginger or turmeric? I find they work better than Tylenol a lot of the time and NO chemicals.

30 **Sarah Howell.** No harm in giving ginger, but we're looking for the fever-reducing attributes of Tylenol. Can't get that from an herbal remedy.

she's been
she's been a trooper

you know[31]
I knew this was a risk when I chose not to immunize
I went into this with eyes wide open and
I'll say it's definitely an inconvenience[32]
but the truth is I'm really enjoying this time we're getting to spend
    together

so I think that might be one way to look at it[33]
you know?
as sort of a gift
a swollen gift to be sure

ELI
*(Putting his phone away and rejoining the conversation he hasn't fully
followed.)*
what do you get for the girl who has everything?[34]

MEIKO
…right

DON
(Off the comments.)
oh-kaaaay

so it seems like there's a
good
conversation underway online
but I am also going to try to keep us moving so

---

31 **Darla Campese.** Actually that's not true. Apple Cider Vinegar, Garlic, Raisin all good for
reducing fever. This has been widely studied.

32 **Terry Nguyen.** We've also been Gluten and Processed Sugar–free since our little guy got
sick and it made a big difference in the swelling.

33 **Darla Campese.** Great suggestion Terry! Also natural nut butters (almond, pistachio) may
help with the aches.

34 **Leslie Kaufman.** [Thumbs-up emoji]

I understand there's been some
miscommunication around [when school is reopening]
so

to be clear
school is closed through Wednesday
and
at that time

only students who
have received the MMR vaccine or
who have already had mumps um
and faculty too
will be able to return
until the quarantine is lifted

so
one thing that is going to happen[35]
we've uh

we're definitely going to have to postpone this year's seventh grade
     a capella concert
because
with about half our students missing there's just no way to rehearse

now the health department is recommending[36] that you get the
     mumps vaccine if you haven't already

but just to be clear
you needed to have had it prior to September 19th to be included
     in the category of people
who are [fine]

to not be affected by the um[37]
quarantine

---

35 **Erin Catlett-Harris.** I made a giant batch of soup and can bring some to anyone who's sick.

36 **Christian Burns.** Wait. HALF the school is antivaxxers? Seriously????

37 **Sandra Blaise.** "Anti-vaxxer" is not really a term I'm comfortable with. It's actually something said out of IGNORANCE.

Don reads comments 36 and 37 and starts to lose his train of thought.

so
uhhhhh

SUZANNE
I think it's worth amplifying that point Don?[38]

DON
um yes
which point?

SUZANNE
even if they *do* get the vaccine now
they still wouldn't
they'd still be forced to stay home[39]

so there's no
there's no tangible benefit to getting it at this point

CARINA
well there is a[40]
I mean isn't the benefit of getting it that then you would have the
    immunity?

SUZANNE
or you can also get a natural immunity from just having the disease

ELI
but for that you have to like[41]
have the disease

---

38 **Christian Burns.** Oh well then Sandra, enlighten away!

39 **Sandra Blaise.** It's easy to call someone crazy if you've never walked a mile in their shoes.

40 **Sandra Blaise.** I wake up every single morning wishing I could go back to being that carefree gluten and sugar–eating person I was 15 years ago.

41 **Sandra Blaise.** But I can't

SUZANNE
of course there's a trade-off
that's why it's so important every family get to make the decision
    that's right for them[42]
right Meiko?

MEIKO
uh yeah no
I mean no one's saying vaccines don't work

ELI
oh okay yeah[43]

MEIKO
like
for what it's worth
if you're saying
have vaccines reduced diseases in the world?[44]
Absolutely
do they largely work at what they're supposed to do?
Absolutely
like, they definitely work[45]

are they the *only* answer?
are they the *best* answer?

for me
that I'm not so sure about[46]

ELI
you just mean like
it's one thing if you're looking at this from a Public Health Perspective

42 **Karen Sapp.** Exactly Sandra! Protect your children by EDUCATING YOURSELVES.

43 **Tyler Coppins.** OR, Protect your children by VACCINATING THEM.

44 **Darla Campese.** You all really feel good about giving 26 shots to a baby in its first year of life?

45 **Sandra Blaise.** And we wonder about the rise in autism, learning differences, allergies etc.

46 **Tyler Coppins.** Thanks for the perspective, Patient Zero!

talking about what's best for Whole Populations

as opposed to maybe
the choices people are making as Individuals[47]

MEIKO
no exactly

CARINA
I'm sorry but
isn't that
isn't that the same thing?[48]

like
isn't the population just made up of a bunch of individuals?

ELI
I think she just means more
it's one thing when it's the 1950s and there's a polio epidemic[49]
in that case

SUZANNE
well there's actually a lot of debate about why we don't see much
      polio anymore
you know they have evidence it had been around since the ancient
      Egyptians[50]

ELI
really?

SUZANNE
oh yeah

47 **Franny Richards.** Not true. She wasn't the first. Get your facts straight!!!

48 **Bryan Serulnek.** Is it fair to have school open if half the kids can't be there? We ALL pay tuition.

49 **Lena Birnbaum-Gerstein.** Wouldn't staying open for only ONE category of kids be a form of discrimination?

50 **Alandra Garcia-Hunt.** Maybe instead of these quarantine days, we could add on some Saturdays when we reopen?

they could tell from the
I think the sarcophaguses?[51]

MEIKO
(To Carina.)
also I think it's just about being humble
you know?[52]

SUZANNE
so
as to why it had a big spike and then went away[53]
it's not so cut and dry

MEIKO
like in the '50s they recommended giving formula instead of breastmilk
because it's easier to digest
which it *is*

SUZANNE
(To Eli.)
hygiene plays a big factor probably[54]

DON
(Off the comments.)
okay okay

MEIKO
(Continuing.)
but now we know how important breastmilk is for building the biota
    of the gut

---

51 **Terry Nguyen.** Or longer school hours?

52 **Sandra Blaise.** Maybe skip spring break?

53 **Terry Nguyen.** Frankly if you're worried about the spread of mumps (which isn't very serious), then EVERYONE should stay home.

54 **Courtney Riley.** Wait what???? Why should we be forced to keep our kids home because you CHOOSE to endanger yours?

and like[55]
how important gut bacteria is if you want to grow up to be like a
Healthy Vibrant Person

DON
(To the livestream audience.)
can we hold for just one second and[56]
I'm just gonna try to get us all back on the same page here

so um
let me just let me just respond[57]
if we can all

(To the group.)
sorry sorry[58]

okay okay um[59]

> *He holds up his hands to try to slow down the online comments.*

just just just[60]
(To the group, and the camera.)
okay
so
I would like to respond directly to
it seems like a few people have brought up the idea of keeping the
    school closed entirely
until the end of the quarantine
and just to be clear[61]
that's not really something we're

55 **Darla Campese.** Actually Courtney, we're CHOOSING to keep our kids safe

56 **Deborah Roth.** Maybe we could use some tuition money for a day camp these weeks?

57 **Erin Catlett-Harris.** Great idea! And also use some for in-home tutoring?

58 **Darrel Creighton-Bolano.** I'd be happy to lead morning yoga sessions.

59 **Christian Burns.** Wait. Why would WE pay for YOUR private tutoring?

60 **Erin Catlett-Harris.** It's in EVERYONE's interest that we don't have half the school falling behind.

61 **Reid Nuzzi.** WHAT????

that the executive committee is not discussing that right now[62]

ELI
no yeah no

SUZANNE
but we could

DON
hmmm?[63]

SUZANNE
I'm not saying we should *do* that
but[64]
isn't that what the C.A.C. is for
to be an open forum for people to Bring Forward ideas

DON
um
I suppose[65]

CARINA
wait I'm sorry
why would we keep the school[66] closed if we don't have to

SUZANNE
well there are a lot of things that we don't *have* to do[67]
that we *choose* to do as a community / because of our [values]

62 **Franny Richards.** DON! How can you make such a HUGE UNILATERAL decision without our input???? That is NOT how we operate!!!!

63 **Alandra Garcia-Hunt.** Shouldn't the school allocate resources EQUALLY?

64 **Tyler Coppins.** CANNOT BELIEVE we are even having this conversation!

65 **Kate Pacyniak.** Typical behavior from the Executive Committee of FASCISM.

66 **Leslie Kaufman.** [Thumbs-up emoji]

67 **Doug Wong.** Okay here's another idea: what if we made the quarantine days OPTIONAL.

CARINA
not everyone can afford three
    weeks of childcare
or taking off work

SUZANNE.
it'd be a burden no question
I'm not suggesting we *do* it
I just think we want to have the
    whole picture

> *Suzanne gives her attention*
> *back to the screen, effectively*
> *ending the conversation with*
> *Carina.*

CARINA
(Responding to Don.)
but also
just from a *fiduciary* [standpoint]
utilities, mortgage, salaries
these are sunk costs, right?[70]

ELI
unless it's like a
a furlough situation?[71]

CARINA
would that even be legal?

ELI
okay so
Don if we did keep it closed[68]
would we end up needing to add
    days onto the end of the year?

DON
well it would depend on how
    long obviously
but
I would imagine so[69]

---

68 **Orson Mankel.** Doug, that's idiotic. If the "problem" is that we won't have enough kids in class, why make the problem worse???

69 **Rivka Rasmussen.** Orson Mankel, please do not call another member of our community an "idiot." We're all just trying to figure this out.

70 **Orson Mankel.** I said the IDEA was idiotic, not him.

71 **Orson Mankel.** Which it is.

SUZANNE
well couldn't it just be like
like closing for the Jewish Holidays[72]

MEIKO
oh
that's an interesting way of [thinking about it]

> *During the following, Eli receives a text, sends a text, receives a text. Texts back and forth anxiously.*

SUZANNE
because I recall
when we made that decision[73]

the thinking behind it was
we didn't want to single out those who would be missing[74]
to make them feel alienated for their religious practice
so closing school on those days was
is
a sign of respect[75]

> *During the following, Meiko notices Eli's texting. Gets his attention. Mouths "Is everything okay?" He nods and waves her off.*

CARINA
I'm sorry
just to
um
isn't it one thing to do it for just one or two days[76]
but a whole other / thing to

---

72 **Orson Mankel.** But I APOLOGIZE if you misinterpreted.

73 **Melanie Alexander.** Great analogy Suzanne!!

74 **Leslie Kaufman.** [Thumbs-up emoji]

75 **Francis Alvarez.** Um, sorry. Religion ≠ vaccine denial

76 **Josephine Lawrence.** Actually Francis, sometimes vaccine refusal does = religion.

SUZANNE
it's a difference of scale maybe[77]

ELI
(Rejoining the conversation, which he'd been half-following.)
but I wonder
isn't it also a matter of
of planning?[78]
of uh
intentionality?

SUZANNE
I'm not sure what you mean[79]

ELI
it's about it's about
it's volitional
stated up front at the beginning of the year[80]
so when you you you *choose* to enroll

MEIKO
you're saying
in the same way you agree[81]
as part of this community
that you're not going to pack nuts of any kind in your child's [lunch][82]

ELI
exactly

---

77 **Josephine Lawrence.** Who are you to question my religious beliefs???

78 **Francis Alvarez.** Ignorance is your religion, Josephine?

79 **Sandra Blaise.** Doesn't it all come down to faith?

80 **Sandra Blaise.** Do you have faith that our bodies were built to handle these kind of pathogens?

81 **Sandra Blaise.** Or faith in Big Pharma?

82 **Darrel Creighton-Bolano.** As a chiropractor, I've seen all sorts of terrible things from Mainstream Medicine.

I mean Tobias *loves* peanut butter and jelly sandwiches[83]
but

DON
(Reading the comments, addressing the camera.)
you know I think we might be getting / a little off [track]

SUZANNE
I hear that Eli[84]
and maybe going forward that's something we're going to want to
    [address]
But
I do think there is a whole set of implicit agreements that are made[85]
when you choose to be part of this community

we couldn't possibly spell out every single assumption

ELI
yeah no for sure but

DON
(To the group.)
can we just pause this conversation for one second and[86]

and
(Reading comment 86, then talking to the camera.)
uh uh okay
let's all just
can I ask everyone who's participating here to just[87]

---

83 **Myla Townes.** Sorry, chiropractors are not doctors.

84 **Terry Nguyen.** Actually chiropractors have way more hours of schooling in anatomy than MDs.

85 **Myla Townes.** If you don't have a JD, you're not a lawyer. If you don't have an MD, you're not a medical doctor. It's that simple.

86 **Orson Mankel.** You want to play Russian roulette with your kids, go for it. But when you bring Little Miss Typhoid Mary to school, you put all our children at risk.

87 **Delia Perez.** You're a disgusting human, Orson Mankel

let's just take our fingers off the keyboards for a second and[88]

okay
let me just say

we truly appreciate you taking part in this
experiment[89]
because that's what it is
this virtual C.A.C.

and I think
and I am absolutely not trying to censor anyone
but I think for this to work[90]
we need to
we need to imagine that everyone is here in the room together
so we can all be part of *one* conversation[91]

okay?[92]

> *Don, in school-teacher mode, waits to confirm the com-*
> *ments have stopped, the way he would when he's waiting for*
> *the class to stop talking. Once he's satisfied they've stopped:*

Okay.

> *From here until Suzanne's "first student to be diagnosed*
> *with mumps," Don gives his attention to the group and*
> *doesn't follow the comments.*

uhhh Suzanne what were you saying?

SUZANNE
I um
I was talking about what are we *choosing*
when we choose to be part of this community

---

88 **Myla Townes.** What's truly disgusting is endangering others people's children over your pseudo-scientific bullshit.

89 **Carlos Banyon.** Let's all take it down a notch guys.

90 **Josephine Lawrence.** Not a guy, sorry.

91 **Tonya Wallace.** Remember what Don said about CONCENTRIC CIRCLES!

92 **Leslie Kaufman.** [Thumbs-up emoji]

what are those values?
and how do we make choices / that align with those [values]

ELI
so but
okay

so isn't part of Making Positive Change in the World
isn't embedded there the idea
that you as an Individual have agency in society
that you have the ability to make choices and your choices have an
    impact on those around you
so isn't that
isn't the second part of that
that Choices Have Consequences

and part of making a choice is embracing those consequences?[93]

DON
would you expand on that?

ELI
sure
I mean
Rebecca and I chose to vaccinate[94]
of course we used the Sears book
the Delayed Schedule
but you know
we made that choice[95]

so now
and as a result
Tobias is now not at risk so

which could be another way to think about it

93 **Dara Konrad.** Heidegger has a great treatise on this concept.

94 **Dara Konrad.** Link: www.nccu.edu/1079/heid_sch.pdf

95 **Sandy Washington.** Dr. Sears is very mainstream. Not anti-vaccine, just thinks maybe we give TOO MANY vaccines

Risk–Reward[96]

we took that risk and now this is the reward
we get to
to have him keep going to school[97]

SUZANNE
oh my god Eli
is that
do we really want to be thinking of our children as a
like your stock portfolio?[98]

CARINA
well maybe it's simpler to just
just at a basic level
why should the students
the ones who *are* immunized[99]

ELI
right
why should they be penalized?
isn't that a sort of Collective Punishment[100]

MEIKO
uh but
punishment implies you did something wrong[101]

---

96 **Christian Burns.** Sears is actually NOT a mainstream doctor. VERY fringe.

97 **Sarah Howell.** Medically there's NO benefit in delaying vaccines or spreading them out beyond the recommended schedule.

98 **Jamila Hayes.** NOT TRUE! Babies immune systems are too fragile to handle 14 viruses.

99 **Arnold Filmore.** The "mainstream" medical literature is ALL funded by Big Pharma.

100 **Leslie Kaufman.** [Thumbs-up emoji]

101 **Darla Campese.** There was just a big article about this community in China or Taiwan where the entire population was forcibly vaccinated and they still had a massive outbreak of Rubella.

DON
right
we would certainly not want to feel like we were
engaging in a form of
punishing the child for the sins of the parent

SUZANNE
can we[102]
can we not?

frame this in terms of *sin* and *punishment*
that makes me *very uncomfortable*

MEIKO
me too actually[103]

DON
you're right
I apologize
that was inappropriate[104]

SUZANNE
because an equally valid frame could be

this is an Unjust System
if the school stays open for only *some* of the students[105]

we're creating a sort of
second class
a sort of Apartheid system
and *who knows* / what kind of far-reaching

CARINA
oh come on

102 **Erin Catlett-Harris.** We went to Beijing last summer and could hardly breath!

103 **Sandra Blaise.** There's SO MUCH corruption in Chinese Pharma!!!!

104 **Arnold Filmore.** Just answer honestly: Would you rather have measles or autism?

105 **Orson Mankel.** Just answer honestly: Were you dropped on your head as a child?

DON
alright let's let's just / try to

SUZANNE
maybe we'll have one water fountain[106] for children who have been
    vaccinated
and one / water fountain for

ELI
that seems a little over the top[107]

SUZANNE
really?

ELI
mmhmmm

SUZANNE
well Eli
tell me this
do you want to bring Tobias over for a playdate at my house
    tomorrow?[108]

ELI
what?

SUZANNE
if you have total confidence[109]

---

106 **Lena Birnbaum-Gerstein.** DO YOUR RESEARCH! There's a whistleblower at the CDC exposing all these vaccine lies.

107 **Christian Burns.** TRUE FACTS: Moonlanding wasn't faked. 9/11 wasn't an inside job. Global Warming is real. Vaccines Don't Cause Autism.

108 **Carlos Banyon.** Can't there be a middle ground? Some vaccines are okay, but maybe not all?

109 **Zane Mercer.** Sorry. In science there's facts and there's lies. THERE IS NO MIDDLE GROUND.

ELI
um
sure
he's been immunized

A moment—maybe a look between Meiko and Eli?

SUZANNE
really?[110]

ELI
yes

SUZANNE
well
you know who else was "immunized"?

the first student to be diagnosed with mumps

DON
SUZANNE!
Suzanne[111]

SUZANNE
I'm not going to say
the child's *name* Don
but people need to
know

Don addresses the camera.

I cannot comment on
WE should not be
commenting on an
individual [student][112]

these vaccines don't
always work

ELI
is that true?

but I can say

---

110 **Karen Stacin.** I saw so many bad things as a nurse. That's why I made the choice that I would NEVER subject my children to Western Medicine.

111 **Reid Nuzzi.** Did you just say you'd NEVER TAKEN YOUR CHILD TO A DOCTOR????????

112 **Karen Stacin.** The best thing I can do for them is leave their bodies PURE.

SUZANNE
maybe someone can
post a link to this online
Merck is currently
being sued for
falsifying data
they lied about the
efficacy of the vaccine
and that's why you're
seeing
around the country
you're seeing most
people who are
getting mumps *have*
been vaccinated[116]

I think I can say[113]
my understanding is
there has been a case
of a student
who *was* vaccinated
contracting[114]
but I think what's
really
what's going to serve
us best here is[115]

*Eli checks his phone,
stands up.*

ELI
sorry excuse me just
one sec

*He walks away from
the group, so he's not
in front of the camera.
Makes a call.*

CARINA
where did you hear
that?
that doesn't seem /
[plausible]

*Don starts catching up
on the comments he
missed. It throws him.*

which is why
which is why

hi yeah

I think you should go

SUZANNE
it's all over the news[117]

MEIKO
(To Carina.)
well there is this
board that gets to
decide which vaccines
are[118] mandatory

yeah no

(To Meiko.)
Exactly! The conflict
of interest is ridiculous

no no just go right
now

---

113 **Tonya Qun.** That's child abuse!!!

114 **Leslie Kaufman.** [Thumbs-up emoji]

115 **Karen Stacin.** When they are adults they can make their own choices about their bodies.

116 **Carlos Banyon.** I'm sorry. As a therapist, I'm a Mandatory Reporter.

117 **Carlos Banyon.** I'm now obliged to call CHILD PROTECTIVE SERVICES

118 **Paula Moody.** THAT was not called for. Don't be such a fucking asshole.

CARINA
I would think if it was all over the news I would have heard about it

SUZANNE
There's a lot of misinformation out there it's hard to navigate it's not your fault

CARINA
excuse me?

SUZANNE
I simply meant you may not have as much education in this area as I do

do you know the number of people who are harmed by a vaccine-preventable disease in the U.S. it's it's it's close to zero

and many of the people on the board also hold patents[119]

Meiko notices Eli has gotten up.

DON
(Still following the online conversation.)
I think we may have[120] and this is of course my fault

Overstepped[121] some initial Ground Rules so[122]

Don reads comment 122.

okay okay
I have said this once and I am going to say it again[123] and I am going to say it
More Emphatically

okay okay
I'm leaving right this second

okay fine no I'll just meet there okay

He hangs up. Walks back.

MEIKO
is everything ok?

ELI
um yeah no
I don't know

MEIKO
what is it?
can I can I [do anything]

ELI
I said IT'S FINE!

---

119 **Josephine Lawrence.** Maybe you'd didn't know this, but Human Beings survived millions of years before Western Medicine.

120 **Myla Townes.** And half of all women died in childbirth!

121 **Darla Campese.** Wake up!!! The answer is not to get another dose of a failed vaccine.

122 **Christian Burns.** Remember that time I got crippled from polio? Oh, no wait. I didn't. Cause I got FUCKING VACCINATED.

123 **Lena Birnbaum-Gerstein.** Your complacency in the destruction of children's lives is disgusting.

CARINA
is it?

SUZANNE
I mean it's for sure it's far less than the one in nine getting asthma from vaccines
or than the one in fifty with a peanut allergy from the Hib vaccine?
or the one in thirty-six getting autism from the MMR

CARINA
Uh what? I don't know where you're getting those numbers from but they seem insanely high

SUZANNE
these are documented facts

if we can't[124]

Don reads the comment.

please THINK that the things you say are going to be taken as[125] examples of
how our community behaves and[126]

From here to the end Don reads and reacts to every comment.

if this is not going to be a *productive* conversation[127]

I am going to ask you all once again to just to STOP TYPING

and take a deep breath[128]
and close your
And to to[129]

(To the group and the camera.)
sorry everybody I have to run
I'll um [get caught up later]

sorry

Eli exits.

Don's "STOP TYPING" grabs Meiko's attention and she goes over to read the comments.

MEIKO
oh my god

---

124 **Tyler Coppins.** What do stupid people and dead people have in common? The dead people don't know they're dead either!

125 **Frances Alvarez.** Maybe IGNORANCE is a communicable disease

126 **Pila Baum.** Sorry but refusing to acknowledge vaccine injury is like the GERMANS circa 1944 claiming that they had no knowledge of the concentration camps.

127 **Tyler Coppins.** Ding ding ding! We have a winner! First Nazi reference.

128 **Josephine Lawrence.** Fuck your cynicism asshole. We're talking about our children's lives.

129 **Lena Birnbaum-Gerstein.** How may of you geniuses are aware that vaccines contain cells from human fetuses?

DON
Picture A Garden
a garden lined with Old, Broken
Stones
130

PICTURE A GARDEN![131]

> *Don raising his voice on "PICTURE A GARDEN" stops*
> *Suzanne and Carina in their conversation, wherever they*
> *are—it's fine if they're not to the end.*
> *They go over to read the comments and are horrified.*
> *Perhaps the characters make some nonverbal vocalizations*
> *in response to what they see.*

and inside that Garden is a Labyrinth[132]

> *Don reads the comments, paralyzed.*

this is[133]
this is [not acceptable][134]

> *Don becomes more and more flustered.*

Okay[135]
Okay
that is really[136]
that is *really* not how we[137]

> *Maybe he's hyperventilating a little.[138]*

130 **Orson Manekl.** If my newborn gets mumps, I'm gonna sue you all into your graves.

131 **Arnold Filmore.** Orson, Are you threatening me?

132 **Guita Lakahni.** We're all threatened by your LUNATIC ANTI-SCIENCE DEATH CULT

133 **Josephine Lawrence.** Do what you want, just keep your POISON off my kids.

134 **Christian Burns.** The only POISON is what's coming out of your TRASH MOUTH

135 **Darrel Creighton-Bolano.** Big Pharma is the REAL death cult

136 **Darrel Creighton-Bolano.** When the revolution comes they'll be first against the wall

137 **Francis Alvarez.** You're a bunch of fucking lunatics

138 **Orson Mankel.** I can't believe my kid goes to school with people whose parents are THIS FUCKING STUPID.

This is *NOT* the kind of language
we use in this community[139]

This is *NOT* how we treat each other[140]

I am

I am

[141]

I am going to
I am going to[142]
Count

To

Three

Uno!
[143]

Dos!
[144]

TRES!
[145]

> *Horrified by the last comment, Don slams the computer shut, cutting off the feed.*
> *A moment. They all look at each other. No one's ever seen Don this riled up before.*
> *Don closes his eyes. Takes a deep breath.*

139 **Lena Birnbaum-Gerstein.** It's no wonder no one wants to play with your kids Orson. Apple=Tree.

140 **Myla Townes.** Let's just expose all the anti-vaxxers to these "mild" diseases. We'd solve overpopulation!

141 **Arnold Filmore.** You just WISHED DEATH on your fellow human beings. Wow.

142 **Leslie Kaufman.** [Shock-face emoji]

143 **Myla Townes.** Natural Selection.

144 **Myla Townes.** Or don't you believe in that either?

145 **Arnold Filmore.** You're an ignorant cunt

Iiiiiii
am feeling

like this format
is not facilitating us all bringing our best selves to this conversation

   Lights.[146]

INTERMISSION

146 See notes on playing this scene in the back of this volume.

ACT TWO

Scene 4

The library. One week later.

Eli enters. Looks around. Sees it's empty. Takes a deep breath. Exits.

He returns with the chairs, unstacks them, and sets them up in a semi-circle.

Meiko enters. Sees him. Stops.

MEIKO
Hey you're uh
you're

here

ELI
uh yeah
yep

> *Meiko goes to him. Gives him a long, deep hug. He hugs her back.*

MEIKO
(While hugging.)
I'm so so sorry

ELI
thanks

> *End hug.*

MEIKO
I've been
I've been texting
I don't know if you've been getting my [texts]

ELI
no yeah
sorry
it's just
it's been

MEIKO
of course

I didn't think you'd be here

ELI
oh I mean uh
I got the email from Don and
seemed important
so

MEIKO
I just mean
I think everybody would understand if you're not feeling up to [this
      meeting]

ELI
oh uh
yeah
um
also probably good to be able to put my mind on something else for
      a minute though
ya know?

MEIKO
of course no yeah
whatever you [need]

          She takes a deep breath, then asks:

how um
how
how's Tobias?

ELI
(First tiny crack in the façade of holding it together.)
he's uh
well
they had him in a
a Medically Induced Coma
so he's
just to
to give his body a chance to um
to fight and

MEIKO
I know I heard
your poor little guy

ELI
but now he's uh
awake and alert
and
stable at the moment
so they're
they're
optimistic

MEIKO
he's
he's gonna be okay

ELI
are you uh
are you asking?

MEIKO
no yeah uh
I meant

ELI
yeah um

yeah

now they're saying there might be some uh
pretty substantial hearing loss
in his
his left ear

> *Meiko makes a nonverbal sound of pain/sympathy.*

but it's gonna be a while
before they know the um
extent

and if it's going to be permanent or

MEIKO
oh my god

> *Meiko hugs him again, this time he doesn't really return it.*
> *During this, Don appears in the entrance, sees them. Turns,*
> *exits.*

how's um
how's Rebecca doing?

ELI
not uhhh
not so great

she hasn't slept in like a week
we're basically living at the hospital
and
she can't sleep when she's with him
finally yesterday I told her
I said
you *must* go home and sleep
so

and shower
and eat

MEIKO
right

Some silence.

are you um
are you hungry?
can I order you some food or

ELI
no no uh

Rebecca doesn't eat when she's [anxious]
whereas I
have completely exhausted the Dorito supply from the hospital's
     third-floor vending machine
the second floor is Touch And Go

MEIKO
I think I have an apple in my bag
maybe some roughage?

ELI
okay
sure

> *Meiko reaches into her bag, pulls out an apple. Hands it to him.*

thanks

> *He crunches a bite.*

I used to think the worst part about being a parent was that every
     fucking cliché is true
you find yourself having these disgusting conversations about
oh *it's all joy and no fun*
the days are long but the years are short
but
I would just sit there in that room staring at him and thinking
I'm so lucky I've gotten to have you in my life
I'm so lucky I've gotten to have you in my life
I'm so lucky I've gotten to have you in my life
and I'm like

why was I so bothered by that

that other people experience the same thing I experience?

A lull.

MEIKO
everybody's been
you know
thinking about you
sending our love

ELI
thanks

what'd you all decide to do about the [school reopening]

I saw a whole big email chain but I couldn't really like
process [it]
or

MEIKO
oh we're gonna
we're just gonna keep the whole school closed for everybody until
    the quarantine is [lifted]

Don just thought
after what happened
a Cooling Off Period might be [a good idea]

ELI
right

but
Olivia's doing okay?

MEIKO
oh she's she's
she's fine she's
pretty much all better

ELI
good

MEIKO
if I had
obviously if I had known

ELI
sure

MEIKO
I just feel so completely [gutted]

ELI
look

there's no way to even be sure he got it from her

MEIKO
but still

      Mini-beat.

ELI
it's not your fault

MEIKO
thank you
for saying that

      Eli crunches the apple.

it's just uh
I think Rebecca might
think it is

ELI
why would you think that?

MEIKO
she uh
she texted me

ELI
what'd she say?

She pulls out her phone.

MEIKO
just
whore

She hands him the phone.

if you keep scrolling up
like
pretty much once an hour just
whore
whore
whore

ELI
(Trying to work out the puzzle.)
hmmmm

(Having solved it.)
she probably just like
copy and pasted

MEIKO
…right

I just
I thought you guys had uh
had
Passed Through Monogamy

ELI
we have
we did
both of us
I am capable of loving more than one person at a time
and so is she and that's

I mean

sure
we generally do try to have it be somebody the other person doesn't
    know
but
she barely knows you so

MEIKO
we were on the development committee last year

ELI
no yeah but
there were a lot of uh [people on it]
it was a huge committee, right?

MEIKO
we co-chaired it

ELI
well look
marriages are [complicated]

it's hard to understand if you've never been in one

MEIKO
(Hurt.)
I've had relationships

ELI
okay
sure

        A moment.

I can
look
I'll ask her to stop texting but

I can't tell her how to feel

MEIKO
it's fine
I mean
if it helps
if it makes her feel better to [take her feelings out on me]
I can ignore it

I just
I just want him to be okay

ELI
(His only moment of actual intentional cruelty.)
well
a little late for that but
thanks

> *Suzanne enters.*

SUZANNE
ooohh Eli

> *She goes and gives him a hug.*

you didn't have to

you know you didn't have to come tonight sweetheart, right?

ELI
oh I know
uh

SUZANNE
and you have just been in all of our hearts

so much

> *Eli realizes he can't handle being here.*

ELI
yeah I wanted to
but
uh

I actually

it turns out
I actually need to
get back to the hospital
(Looking at Meiko.)
be with my family

SUZANNE
oh
of course

ELI
sorry I couldn't stay

SUZANNE
(Taking his hand in hers.)
you need anything you call me okay

ELI
yeah uh

SUZANNE
I mean it

ELI
thanks

sorry um

> *Eli glances at Meiko, they make eye contact for a second*
> *before he breaks it.*
> *He starts to leave as Don enters with Carina.*

DON
Eli!

I didn't think you'd / [be here]

ELI
hey Don
um

Eli tries to go but is sort of blocked by Don.

DON
com'ere my friend.

Don gives him a big hug.

ELI
sorry I can't um

Eli gently wiggles out of the hug.

it turns out I gotta go

DON
oh

ELI
so

Eli gets past Don, sees Carina.
A tiny of moment of "is she gonna hug him too, or is he able to escape?"
He diverts with a little wave. She waves back. He exits.
A moment of awkward quiet.
Don goes and sits in one of the chairs and gestures for the rest to join him.

DON
would you all mind just? [joining me here]

Everyone sits in the chairs Eli has set up.

thank you
and now if we could
as a way to enter the space together
can I ask you all to just
close your eyes and take a deep breath and

Don closes his eyes, and takes a deep breath. On the second breath, Suzanne joins him with the closed eyes and deep breath.
Carina joins on the third.
Meiko doesn't. Instead, she gets out her needles and starts knitting anxiously.

After the third breath, Don opens his eyes.

great
and now
let's all go around and each say one word about where we're landing
    right now
don't think
just [speak]

    Don looks at Suzanne.

SUZANNE
fragile

DON
(Nodding.)
mmmmmm

    Don turns his gaze to Carina.

CARINA
ummmm
concerned?

DON
thank you

    Don turns his gaze to Meiko. She's checked out and it takes
    her a beat to realize everyone's attention is on her.

MEIKO
oh
uh

pass

    A small moment. Don clocks that something is weird here,
    but decides to ignore it.

DON
okay

    Don widens his gaze.

for me it's
grateful

93

because you know
this has been the most trying span of days in my whole work-life
and

I'm so *grateful* that I have been able to draw such strength from each
    of you
so
Thank You

SUZANNE
of course Don

DON
and
I want to acknowledge that we're all feeling a lot of anxiety
for Eli
for his family
and also
for our community as a whole

I think it goes without saying
that we have a great deal of work to do
to uh
to rebuild trust
so

given all that I think what's best
all we can do at the moment is to uh

to focus on
what we can [do]
on the positive
on what we can
do

SUZANNE
of course

DON
so

94

our first item here is uh
I assume some of you are aware
there's a
petition?
floating around
asking that uh
families pledging that
they will not return to the school unless we
until such time as we
revise our
the school's
Immunization Policy

MEIKO
in what way?

DON
to uh
it would be
to start requiring vaccinations
as a uh
as a condition of / returning to school

SUZANNE
well that is

MEIKO
when they return next
      week or when they
      return next year?

I'm sorry I don't know why we're
that is obviously a nonstarter

CARINA
I think it's
as soon as we
as soon as we reopen

DON
I completely understand that you
      [feel that way]
(To Carina and Meiko.)
that is my understanding
yes

MEIKO
and is this ALL vaccines or just the MMR?

SUZANNE
I think what Meiko's saying and I agree is this is not the kind of thing
    that we can / just suddenly *decide*

MEIKO
(Lashing out.)
I can speak for myself thank you!

> *A tiny moment. Everyone is a little taken aback.*

Don?

DON
my understanding is it's the
the standard ones
the Recommended Schedule

SUZANNE
well first
I think we need to recognize that there's a very good chance that
    this whole thing is is
is
it's
what's the word
trolling?
someone who was probably
understandably
upset by the online conversation
is now
they're trolling
they trying to Sow Chaos
and perhaps the best response is just to
Not Engage

rather than letting ourselves be dragged down in the mud by one
    angry person
we just

96

When They Go Low We Go High

(To Carina.)
right?

      A tiny moment.

CARINA

…

DON
okay
so it's
it's not just *one* person
there's um
it's upwards of fifty families last I checked
and?   MEIKO
                                          five-zero?

yes and also just context
I went ahead and did a little back-of-the-napkin math
and if we were to lose even half that many families
at this point in the year?

SUZANNE
what about the cash reserves?

DON
this is including [the cash reserves]
the bathroom conversion has really eaten up / a lot of the

SUZANNE
okay well
what if we
let's just take things one step at a time
make sure we have all our ducks in a row to reopen next week
and we'll see how many of these people actually don't [come back]
because I don't believe that *twenty-five*
families are going to to   DON
[not come back]   well it's it's actually [fifty]
and *then*

if it turns out we need to do a little extra fundraising this year
then we will
we will
Make It Work
just as we always do

DON
okay
and
if that is the consensus view then then then

but but
I do feel obligated to point out that the
the petition was also signed by a member of the executive committee

so

MEIKO
what did he uh
what did he say?
is he / going to

SUZANNE
look
Eli is experiencing a trauma
and I know
I know better than most
in a moment like that you
you lose the ability to think rationally
you are looking
you are just so desperately looking for someone to blame
and I think it requires from all of us
to extend our sense of of of   DON
                                                 so it was not uh

empathy?
                                                 Eli was not

and /
and   the person who

98

oh

oh

      A little moment.

CARINA
I'm sorry
I wasn't trying to be uh
deceptive?

I just didn't want to make this about my personal [point of view]

this is a petition from the community
so I think we have an obligation to [consider it]
right?

but honestly I do feel like in light of what's happened
that that

and
a number of parents have reached out to me
so it's not just my feelings
it's about
it's about
someone needs to advocate for / for [their point of view]

SUZANNE
this is

Carina
you are new to our community
and you are welcome here
we appreciate what you bring

but there are things that are are
fundamental
to what makes our community
our community

do you know what I mean?

CARINA
ummmm

SUZANNE
so it's it's it's

CARINA
I don't

SUZANNE
what?

CARINA
I don't know what you mean

SUZANNE
well
okay

uh
for one thing
if we
changed
this policy

there wouldn't be a place in this school for my family anymore
or Meiko's family
a lot
a lot
of people
they would leave
and then like Don said
there wouldn't be any school left for you to be a part of
so
is that what you want?

CARINA
of course not

SUZANNE
cause that is *exactly* what you're asking

DON
okay okay
let's just [pause]

    A little moment.

this is Hard Stuff folks
let's just all take a moment to acknowledge that

and also
let's make sure we keep as our baseline
that everybody here is operating out of the best of intentions

SUZANNE
no you're right Don

Carina
I apologize
I did not mean to attack you   CARINA
                     oh I didn't feel uh

you know

                     attacked

I've found that
in situations like this
it can sometimes be helpful to
if we back up and
rather than beginning from our *positions*
that we begin with our
interests?
because we may find there's a lot more overlap than we were aware of

DON
one hundred percent agree

and I can just begin by saying that
my interest
is in having a Thriving School Community

SUZANNE
agree

CARINA
uhhhgreee

> *They look to Meiko. She's knitting.*

DON
Meiko?

MEIKO
uh yeah no
agree

DON
great

SUZANNE
and um
my interest
is in having a place
where all our families can feel welcome and safe

DON
agree

MEIKO
agree

CARINA
I agree

> *Don and Suzanne look to Meiko.*

MEIKO
uhhhh
honesty?
I think we could really use A LOT MORE honesty
in this community
that's uh

> *Meiko drops whatever she was going to say and focuses intensely on her knitting.*

A little moment where they all take in that something is off.
Don once again decides to push forward.

DON
surrrrre

everything we do here is built on honesty
absolutely

CARINA
agree

SUZANNE
agree

DON
okay
oh
you know what?
we should really be
we should really be [writing these down]
(Does a "writing on a whiteboard" gesture.)
sorry just one moment

> *Don exits quickly.*
> *Some silence. Meiko knits. Suzanne gives Carina a little smile.*
> *Carina pulls out her phone and starts scrolling through it.*
> *Suzanne waits, then:*

SUZANNE
Meiko
it's so great that Eli has you in his life right now

MEIKO
hmmmm?

SUZANNE
that you're able to...
be there for him
to lean on

Meiko looks up again.

MEIKO
oh uh
you know we haven't really been in touch

that much

SUZANNE
oh?

MEIKO
he's been
you know
he's been pretty [preoccupied]

SUZANNE
(Nodding.)
sure

I just
I would've thought *you* would've

    A little moment.

MEIKO
(Kind of snaps at her.)
I think probably their family just needs a little space right now

SUZANNE
of course

    Some more silence.

CARINA
oh!
I brought some
I brought scones!
from the place

    Carina pulls out a little bag of scones.

SUZANNE
that's so thoughtful

Carina pulls out some disposable plates. She gestures for them to help themselves.

CARINA
they're gluten-free

They don't.

SUZANNE
but you know we don't
we don't bring disposable plates on campus

CARINA
no no these are
recycled, biodegradable, totally organic

SUZANNE
but still
as far as setting an example

CARINA
right right
I
I did the research
this company claims
and with the drought?
it's actually *better* for the environment than using a dishwasher

MEIKO
(Not looking up from her knitting.)
that seems like a dubious claim

CARINA
I'll send you both the link

SUZANNE
perfect

They all sit there a while.

Don enters with a giant Post-it Note pad on an easel.

DON
okay!

He uncaps a marker.

Here
We
Go

He writes the word "INTERESTS."

(As he does.)
In-ter-ests

He glances back, sees the scones.

ooo
scones!

He picks one up and eats it during the following:

(As he writes them on the sheets.)
Thriving Community

Safe & Welcome

Honesty

He briefly admires his work.

beautiful

okay

Carina?
did you want to

CARINA
um
safety also for me?

Don puts a check mark next to "SAFE & WELCOME."

DON
great

okay

another one for me would be just
Keeping the Lights On
even without losing any students
just the fact that we've had to add days onto the end of the school
    year is going to
there'll be a *crunch*
so

      He starts to write "FISCAL RESPONSIBILITY."

CARINA
do we need to
do you think we need to
um

clarify	DON
at all	oh no
	I think at this stage we're just

what we mean by
I don't know if we're   sorry
[using words to mean the same thing]   I didn't meant to cut you off
                                       go on

well just
with *safety*
I meant like
specifically

in this context I think that really
    means
making sure no one is at risk of uh

                            mmmhmmm

which would mean
that we have enough students who *are* immunized
so that we can achieve
Herd Immunity
which is you know
the concept that / you need to have a certain [percentage of people
    immunized]

107

SUZANNE
we know what Herd Immunity is

CARINA
right so
from what I understand
the mumps vaccine is eighty-eight percent effective
so that's why everyone needs to get it
so that the Herd Immunity can protect the other twelve percent
like Tobias
for whom it / doesn't work

SUZANNE
actually it's the mumps vaccine that's preventing the natural herd
    immunity from being able to take its course

CARINA
I don't
I'm sorry
I'm not sure where you got that from
but I don't think that's true

DON
okay okay okay
I'm gonna ask that we just table this for a [moment]

right now we're focused on
Common Interests

        Tiny beat.

SUZANNE
Respect
Don
would be a big one for me

DON
sure
I think we can all [agree]
that's a

(As he writes "RESPECT.")
Core
Val
You

> *Don waits for Carina or Meiko to chime in. They don't.*

DON
(Prompting.)
agree?

CARINA
uh
I think so

SUZANNE
and since we're *clarifying*?

by that I mean that
none of us has the right to tell another person that their point of
    view is
Not Valid

DON
absolutely
(As he writes it.)
ALL POV = VALID

great

uh
Meiko?

CARINA
I'm uh
I'm not sure that I agree

DON
I'm sorry?

CARINA
I just
I mean like
everyone's point of view is not equally valid like
All of the Time
like if I say the Moon is Made of Cheese
then obviously

DON
um

SUZANNE
no
of course that's true
obviously

CARINA
or
that the earth is flat
which there are actually people out there who who [believe]
seriously
there's like all these YouTube videos /
and

SUZANNE
thank you

my point was simply
that when there's phenomena about which there's a lot of
Genuine Scientific Disagreement
that we approach each other with a sense of of
humbleness
as in
I know you're an intelligent, educated woman
so even if I have a different perspective on this
I can't just dismiss what you think out of hand
because then I would be dismissing *you*

and if someone as smart as you feels so strongly
then it's worth me listening with an open mind

CARINA
yeah no but um

DON
okay okay

and I appreciate that

this is a really

but I'm actually / just trying to

this is a very productive I think uh
a good start

DON
I wonder if maybe
with your permission
we let this sit for now
I think we've got a good list going of [interests]
we can just start with the ones that we all [agree on]

> He circles "THRIVING COMMUNITY," "HONESTY," and
> "FISCAL RESPONSIBILITY."

and we can move on to to to

brainstorming some options

> He flips to another sheet.

for actions we can take
that are for
everyone's benefit

(As he's writing at the top of the new sheet.)
Mutual Benefit

Okay
so

we know
we know
that in any circumstance we are going to be under some financial
    strain
so I wonder if

111

if we
we could spitball a list of some
fundraising activities or or or
Suzanne maybe some alumni donors who would
uh

> *They all sit. Don waits expectantly.*

okay well one idea is
is anyone familiar with the concept of a Phantom Ball?
it's where you
you send out invitations
it's just like a regular fundraiser
but you
you don't actually hold the event
that's the Phantom part!
people still buy tickets
they still / make pledges

SUZANNE
look Don
if we need money
we can ask Eli for money

DON
uhh
I'm not sure that's a [road we can go down]

SUZANNE
he's offered before
we can
we can name the bathrooms after him

CARINA
I thought he was a Stay At Home Dad

SUZANNE
yes
and also

like the twelfth employee at Google

MEIKO
Facebook

SUZANNE
whatever
he can afford it

DON
it's not about
it's not about his means
it's

I
would not feel comfortable

his family is going through a very difficult [time]
this is not an appropriate moment to be

SUZANNE
no of course
it would have to be handled

delicately

DON
absolutely
(Considering.)
buuuuut

you are right
he has been very generous in the past and

SUZANNE
he has

DON
and if it's a matter of
Can We Keep the Doors Open

SUZANNE
exactly

> *A little moment. Don hesitates, knowing maybe he shouldn't*
> *do this, but:*

DON
I wonder
would that
would that be something you would feel comfortable broaching
  with him Meiko?

MEIKO
Jesus Christ!

> *Meiko knits VERY AGGRESSIVELY.*
> *A moment.*

DON
okay uhhh

maybe this is a good place to move on to

> *Don flips to another sheet.*

we can just go straight into

(As he's writing at the top of the sheet.)
Action Steps

CARINA
I'm sorry
I'm feeling very unclear about where we are with the
the petition
I mean
this is /
this is all [useful]

DON
I think we're
In Process

SUZANNE
I will say
what's really coming into focus for me here is that
Carina
that we're not going to solve this today
and of course if we don't have a consensus
then there's no way we can make a change in the school's Official Policy
right?

DON
technically that's right

CARINA
okay um
right

can I just ask though
and maybe this is a bad analogy but
does the
does the school have a policy
an Official Policy
on the Teaching of Evolution?

SUZANNE
oh come on

DON
uhhh
not a
we don't
we don't have a *policy*
we teach science, biology

CARINA
right right but I just mean
if there was a
a *creationist* family
then / what would be our

SUZANNE
okay no please
that's offensive

CARINA
can I just
can I please /
can I finish

SUZANNE
not if you're going to
then no I don't think / we need to hear

MEIKO
just say what you're going to say!

CARINA
thank you

I'm just
I'm just trying to understand
if there's a
a Widely Held Scientific View
like say
about evolution

if a family
at home
if they want to believe something different
that's their right I guess
but that doesn't mean we
because we might offend them
that doesn't mean we don't teach it, right?

SUZANNE
well

in your
your

as I said *offensive*
analogy
then I think
if ideas about evolution came in the form of a needle that might
    poison them?
then I think
yes
I think we would reconsider whether / it would be right to [inject a
    student]

CARINA
okay fine
what about
how about
climate change?

like the science is completely settled
there's no / actual debate

SUZANNE
well
it is
it *is* like climate change
that's a *good* analogy
in that
in that
on one side
you have this very powerful
very wealthy industry
paying scientists to doctor their research
and
totally unwilling to acknowledge any data that would threaten /
    their profits

CARINA
but if ninety-nine point nine percent of scientists agree / that it's
    real then

SUZANNE
and on the *other* side you have a
what began as a totally grassroots movement of people saying
hey what you're doing has consequences
and we will no longer let our environment or our children's bodies
	be destroyed
just so you can make more money for your shareholders

CARINA
the the the government
the
you realize the CDC doesn't have shareholders

SUZANNE
who do you think funds the studies?
the pharmaceutical companies

I mean have you been reading any of these stories about how the
	life expectancy among working-class men in the Midwest is
	plummeting and addiction is *skyrocketing*
and it's all from prescription painkillers
because the pharmaceutical companies have
for years
have been pushing doctors to prescribe them
and they're *highly addictive*
because there were studies published in *mainstream* medical journals
saying you know
painkillers aren't addictive
that's how they got the doctors to keep [prescribing them]
and the studies were funded by Big Pharma
this isn't *fringe*
this was in the New Yorker!

so when these same companies come to us and say
we'd like to inject a disease into your one-day-old baby
to prevent an STD
which they *do*
they give a hepatitis B vaccine to newborns

I mean
no thank you!

> *A moment.*

DON
maybe
maybe what we should have done from the outset is just to
just to stipulate up front that
none of us in this room are scientists and
no one here is the Arbiter of Absolute Truth
but each of us / does hold *a* truth

SUZANNE
you know we have talked so much this past year about Implicit Bias
I am feeling a lot of
particularly from you Don

DON
what?

SUZANNE
a very strong bias against people who support parental choice
and I think it's undergirding everything you say
I'm surprised by it
and honestly?
Very Very Disappointed

DON
Suzanne
I know this is a very sensitive issue for you
I am sorry if you're feeling attacked
that was not my intention

SUZANNE
there is no benefit in exploring an idea that would
and this isn't hyperbole
Destroy The School
just because

and frankly I'm not sure that it's appropriate that people who are here
only here
because of the Significant Financial Support the school is providing
    them / should be dictating

DON
hey
that is OUT OF LINE!

    A moment.

SUZANNE
you're right
I apologize

CARINA
I'm not on financial aid

SUZANNE
oh
uh

CARINA
we're a Full-Pay Family

SUZANNE
Oh
yes no
of course

                    DON
                    Iiiiiiiiiiiiiiiiii
                    am very uncomfortable
                    with this discussion
                    we do not
                    discuss a family's [financial
                    status]

I'm sorry
I must've
I must've mixed you up with [someone else]

CARINA
did you?

                              that is
                              that is *really* not
                              [appropriate]

SUZANNE
I I I
did not mean to imply
I would *never*

                              let's uh

CARINA
no of course you wouldn't

                              let's uh
                              let's uh
                              let's
                              see if we can
                              refocus

SUZANNNE
I am so embarrassed

I mean this is no excuse
but I'm just *so* [distraught about everything]

CARINA
I'm sure you are

                         refocus our um [discussion]

        A little moment.

DON
okay um
uh

        *Don casts about for where to go next. Looks around the room
        desperately.*

how about uh
what about

And lands on:

Meiko?

we haven't uh
this might be a nice time to hear your perspective
if you would be uh
willing to uh [offer it]

I for one would love to hear your thoughts

> *Meiko waves him off.*

this is an *open* room
whatever you're thinking is perfectly [appropriate]

> *When Meiko opens her mouth she only intends to say a
> word or two. But once she gets started it all just continues to
> spill out of her, and she can't stop it.*

MEIKO
I think
okay
I think we just have so much *fucking* hubris, you know?

coming out of World War II
and
this sort of industrial revolution
and factory approach to food and food products
and the creation of *plastics*
the move towards this sort of
car
and suburbia
and all this *stuff*
all this stuff that we thought was *so* great

and then it turns *out*
a lot of these marvels of technology
now we realize
there's quite a few of them that we're like
maybe we *shouldn't* be pumping carbon dioxide into the air by the ton
maybe we *shouldn't* be giving our animals antibiotics every five seconds

and

oh shit plastic's really bad for you
it's doing all this terrible stuff to the environment
all this stuff that we thought we wanted
we thought would make us *so* happy
it turns out
we didn't really know the first thing about it!

> *Meiko is on the verge of tears. No one else is quite sure what's*
> *going on.*
> *Is she done talking?*
> *After an awkward beat, Don decides she probably is, and*
> *that someone needs to say something. He opens his mouth to*
> *speak, but then:*

and and and there's all this new research?
about
they said that by looking at people's poop
they can tell
at any point in your life
if you're eighty, if you're twenty, if you're five
they can tell if you've ever had antibiotics anytime in your whole
    entire life
because when you take antibiotics One Time
there are good bacteria that die off and Never Come Back

and they're like
they're like
we don't *know* if this is important yet or not
we're *just now* discovering this

and so it's like
We Fucked Up
with antibiotics
and and so
maybe doing things in a new way isn't always good just because it's new

I get so many things wrong
I get so many things wrong
and
I Don't Know
I Don't Know

123

okay?

I *believe* in Human Fallibility.
like We Could Be Getting This Wrong!

> *Meiko storms out of the room, not wanting to break down in front of everyone.*
> *A weird moment.*

DON
Uhhhh
do you think she's [okay]?

> *No response.*

I think I should uh

> *He points to where she went.*

maybe I should go see if she's [okay]

excuse me just one [second]

> *Don exits.*
> *They sit for a while. Suzanne gives Carina a smile. She gives her a tight smile back.*
> *They look to see if Don's coming back.*
> *He doesn't.*
> *After a bit...*

SUZANNE
I am really really sorry

CARINA
okay

SUZANNE
that's not
that's not who I am
I would
I would *never* [make a racist assumption]

CARINA
well [but you did]

Some silence.

SUZANNE
you know Don
has so many wonderful qualities

he's amazing at connecting with people and
so inspiring
and the children *adore* him
but he's not always
he's a great captain until you come up on an iceberg
ya know?

      Carina picks up her phone.

CARINA
sorry
I just need to check my [email, text messages, etc]

      She starts doing something on her phone.

SUZANNE
oh no
of course

      Carina is on her phone. Suzanne waits for her to finish.
      It goes on for a while.
      Suzanne realizes she's not going to stop, so decides to jump in.

and gosh I hope you know how much respect I have for you
I really do
for how thoughtfully you're engaging with this
and that you that you are
representing a point of view that is
worth hearing from

CARINA
look
I'm just trying to be a [responsible board member]
to do my Due Diligence
okay?

SUZANNE
right no
of course

me too

CARINA
sure

> *Carina goes back to her phone. Suzanne waits a beat. Tries again.*

SUZANNE
you know
it may not seem like it
but I know where you're coming from
I

my grandfather was a doctor
a family doctor
my dad's dad
so

growing up in our house it was
you respected
God
then Doctors
then
Long Spacious Gap
everybody else

> *Carina senses Suzanne is looking for a response.*

CARINA
(Barely looking up.)
mmmm

SUZANNE
yeah you did not go against what my grandfather said
and that remained true all the way through
he lived to a hundred and eight!

good genes right?

Suzanne waits for a response, gets none.

yeah he passed away when I was pregnant with my first
so
never got to meet her

> *Through the following, Carina occasionally looks up and gives just enough attention to not be completely rude, while also doing the "pretend I suddenly have to respond to these Very Important emails/texts" thing.*

it's too bad
he would've loved her
she was this absolutely precious perfect little girl
Juniper was
she was just full of smiles and pure joy
and *so* smart
she was you know
she said her first word at eight months
and was walking at ten months
and was just
so far ahead of all the kids
we used to joke
our joke was
because she's such a genius
we're lucky she's so good-natured
at least she'll be a benevolent dictator!

CARINA
(Just the bare minimum to not be totally rude.)
right

> *At some point during what follows, Carina starts really listening.*

SUZANNE
and then you know
we went in for the
the one-year shots
we didn't think about it
it's what you do

of course

that's when they give you the Live Viruses

to a One-Year-Old

and she just
from the minute she got them she WAILED
and WAILED
her skin was on fire
she cried nonstop for two days
and we would hold her and she would look at us
and she was begging
you could see she was just
she couldn't understand why we couldn't make it better

and I kept calling and calling
and the doctor said
that's normal
that can happen
nothing to worry about
just give some Tylenol for the fever

and finally she stopped crying
but the next day
and the day after that
we realized
she's not talking anymore
she's not even babbling

and we brought her in to the doctor
and he said

nothing to worry about
sometimes there's a regression
it'll pass

and she also
you know she'd been sleeping through the night since five months
but now she was back to
being up every three hours

and finally after about two weeks
we went to bed

128

we were fucking exhausted of course
and I closed my eyes
and when I opened them it was morning
and I thought
I nudged Sam
I was like
did you do the whole night?
and he was like
no I didn't get up

and there was a moment of
ah thank god she's back to sleeping through the

and it was just that one moment
because then I
I
I
Just Knew

and I ran into her room
and she was

CARINA
oh god

SUZANNE
she was so still
so perfect

and she didn't look that different than when

but

CARINA
I'm so sorry

SUZANNE
yeah well
that's what they said too

the doctors

they did a
an
autopsy
they said

Oh it certainly wasn't the vaccine

it was Just SIDS

JUST

that's all

run of the mill

but I KNOW

CARINA
I can't imagine

SUZANNE
no
you can't

because it's like
it's like
and it's like if you went skiing
and you fall and break your leg
and when you go to the hospital and tell them what happened
they say
oh that's crazy
no one ever breaks their leg skiing
it must just be a coincidence
and you think you're losing your mind
and then you go online
and you find a hundred thousand people who have also broken
    their legs while skiing
and also been told by their doctors it must've been something else

and they are also tired of being told they're crazy

    A moment.

CARINA
look

I do really wish that there was a way that this could work out for
	both of us
for all of us

SUZANNE
oh me too

I'm not
I'm not trying to change your mind
I don't think that's my place

but you
you understand why I could never

CARINA
no yeah
of course

SUZANNE
so maybe what we do is
we just
let's just take a day or two and
sleep on it
I've found
sometimes if you just take a step back

it turns out things aren't as impossible as they seem   CARINA
                                                                                                                right

and then
we can start fresh
we can put our heads together and just really figure out
you know
how do we do what's best for the whole community?

	Lights.

Scene 5

The library. Suzanne and Don.

DON
no no no
you're thinking of Marty Berman's wife
the Vegan Chef

SUZANNE
oh my god
the Infamous Cashew Lasagna

DON
it was not
she claims
to this day
she claims
it was not the Lasagna

SUZANNE
it was the Lasagna Don
trust me
the amount of vomit I cleaned up that day?

DON
wait
what did we do
what did we *do*
for lunches the rest of that year?

SUZANNE
you don't remember?

DON
I am drawing a Total Blank

SUZANNE
Theresa McClellan and Jamila Hayes and *Floyd*
do you remember Floyd?

DON
Floyd!

SUZANNE
the clown?

DON
he was a mime actually

SUZANNE
are you sure?

DON
yes he had a
a mime school in Alameda?

did you ever see him perform?

SUZANNE
no

DON
his work was
it was actually quite subtle
he had a certain *something*

SUZANNE
so they would come over to my house at four thirty A.M.
and we would make lunch for everyone for the day
every day

DON
I had completely forgotten about that
how did you *do* it?

SUZANNE
I have no idea

DON
well
you were young

SUZANNE
I was young-*er*

DON
I wonder if that mime school is still going?
I always thought
once I retire

SUZANNE
Don
in ten years
I've never heard you be silent for more than two minutes

DON
exactly

      Carina enters.

CARINA
hi

I'm so sorry
am I late?

SUZANNE
no
not at all

CARINA
great

SUZANNE
sit
sit

CARINA
oh sure

> *Carina sits.*

DON
thanks for coming

CARINA
of course

> *A little moment.*

DON
you know I was thinking this morning about
this family
seven eight years ago
they'd just moved from the East Coast
the father was a big-time Sociologist
he'd won a MacArthur genius thing
gotten a job at Cal
and the student, Simon, had been in a
a very Buttoned Up Manhattan Prep School type [place]
and had A LOT of trouble adjusting

and was lashing out at Ronald Stillman
the math teacher
being very aggressive

and we brought in the parents for a meeting
and they were expecting
I could tell
for me to come down Very Hard on their child

but I told them
I said

Simon is doing exactly what Simon is supposed to be doing
taking into account age and experiences
which was not to say we condoned Simon's behavior
or that Simon didn't need to apologize
but the important point was

and this was when it crystallized
We Do Not Turn Our Children Into Villains

and that's really become a bedrock for me of what we do here

and
I know this may be a difficult conversation
but I'm gonna ask that we hold on to that idea
no one in this room is a villain
and we all want what's best for the school

SUZANNE
absolutely

DON
okay
great

       Don waits. Some silence.

SUZANNE
I can
I can start
if that's okay

CARINA
uh
sure

SUZANNE
I had a thought
which was
what if we created a network?

for all the families that choose not to vaccinate

and if one child becomes symptomatic
or if there's an outbreak in the region
we could all
we could codify it
we would
proactively
keep our children home until the whole thing passes

would that
would that [satisfy you?]

CARINA
I
I
I'm sorry but

SUZANNE
hmmm?

CARINA
it's just
that wouldn't really
it wouldn't really solve the [problem]

SUZANNE
okay well
that was just one idea

I am open
we are open to hearing any [idea you have]

because I want to accommodate
I really do
I've been doing a lot of thinking about what you said
and soul-searching

CARINA
me too
I mean

I've been doing a lot of thinking
and reading

SUZANNE
that's great

CARINA
there's a
there's a lot of information out there

SUZANNE
there is *so much*

CARINA
and like
I'm not an expert

SUZANNE
of course

CARINA
but I keep thinking about this
um

(Steels herself to say this.)
have you heard of
do you know about the Vaccine Court?

SUZANNE
(Cautiously.)
I do

CARINA
(Explaining to Don.)
it was set up so that
if someone *is* injured by a vaccine
from an allergy or [something else]
to adjudicate

and compensate

(Back to Suzanne.)
and
there was a
I read about
a famous case
it was like the Test Case for
a family that said their child got autism from the MMR
and they testified how before the vaccine she was absolutely normal
in every way
developmentally
and then as soon as she got it
all these things started happening

SUZANNE
it's very common

CARINA
right so
but here they had to
because it was a court
to like
Present Evidence
and it turned out

there were notes
Doctor's Notes from the
the six-month checkup and the nine-month checkup saying
"this could be something to watch out for"
"this could be an early indication *of…*"
and the parents they just
they had no memory of this and they
that's the thing
I don't think they were lying
I think they
I think their pain was absolutely real
I think they one hundred percent believed what they were saying

but our memories are such unreliable things
especially when there's been a trauma / and

SUZANNE
okay [stop]

CARINA
and I have no doubt
that you absolutely believe what happened
happened just the way you say it did /

SUZANNE
okay okay [stop]

CARINA
but it doesn't change what the science says
it doesn't change what the facts say

and I know
I know it's complicated
but I mean it's also a
it's a
for me
it's a Social Justice Issue
like if
even if
you feel like the choice is
a choice between
doing what's right for your child and what's right for the community?

and I think that's a false choice
but if that's what it is and what we're saying is
I'm not willing to subject my child to even the tiniest amount of risk
so that we can protect people's elderly parents with cancer
or
or
the younger sibling of a student

is that really a community you'd want to be a part of?

A long moment.

DON
can I just acknowledge how much I appreciate / both of you

SUZANNE
(Holding up a hand to cut him off.)
Don Don just

   Don stops talking.

why do you send your child to private school?

CARINA
what?

SUZANNE
why do you send your child to private school?

CARINA
because it's, it's the best environment for / [our son]

SUZANNE
no of course
but just from a
from a Social Justice Perspective
wouldn't the most equitable thing be
if we all went to public school

CARINA
yes
probably

SUZANNE
because there's no question
the schools would improve radically
the pressure that would be exerted to fund them better
I mean can you imagine?

CARINA
you don't send your children to public school

SUZANNE
no
because I
and I won't apologize for it
I believe my first responsibility is to *my children*
and so do you

CARINA
no yeah
you're right
it's just

look
I'm sorry

SUZANNE
no listen
I am sorry

if you feel so strongly
if you stand by that petition
and you choose to leave the school then
then I am sorry we couldn't find a way to make you feel
like there's a place for you here
I really am   CARINA
                                               oh uh

I'll be honest
it makes me feel like a failure
like our
process is a failure
but

                              I'm uh I'm uh not sure [what's
                                   going on]
we're gonna have a really tough year ahead
but we're gonna make it
I know we will

and if you decide
obviously it's not entirely up to me
but if you decide at some point that you want to come back

I'll do my best to make sure that our doors are always open for you

CARINA
oh
okay um

I have to say I'm a little uh [confused]

Don

didn't you
didn't you
talk to her?

DON
Iiiiiiiiii
am only here to facilitate

> *Suzanne looks at Don, back to Carina.*

SUZANNE
…?

CARINA
(Processing.)
uhhhh
okay

um
well
I
you should know
I had a conversation with Eli

SUZANNE
great

CARINA
and uh
he said he's willing to uh
to support us financially
however we need

SUZANNE
(Her antennae are up.)
uh-huh

CARINA
on the
on the
condition that we
change our policy

     A moment.

SUZANNE
I see

did you
did you know about this
this
scheme Don?

DON
let's remember
No One Here Is A Villain

SUZANNE
oh my god

CARINA
I'm really really sorry
I thought he had already uh /

SUZANNE
Don
it is

it is
are you really okay with someone just showing up out of the blue
    and starting to dictate how my
how *our* school / is going to [be run]

DON
Suzanne

no one is dictating anything
obviously
there can't be any change to our policy without a consensus
this is just a discussion
it's one proposal

SUZANNE
well
I don't know what you said to Eli
who knows where his head is at
but I don't see my position changing
or Meiko's position
so

CARINA
actually I've
I've talked to Meiko and and she and Eli and I we're
we're all on the same page about this I think
and I'm sorry
I know this puts you in the most awful position but I think
it's like you said

we have to put the community first
right?

>   *Lights.*

Scene 6

The library. Don stands, holding his Rumi book.

Eli, Meiko, Carina, and Winter seated around the child-sized tables. As the new person, Winter is seated in the middle.

The bookshelf that contained Suzanne's books is empty.

DON
so
as some of you know
I always like to close out the first executive committee meeting of
    the year
with a little passage from Rumi
which is

> *He holds an old paperback book and reads from it.*

The world was a night, and we, travelers in the dark
Till the sun arose and cried
"Begone, Oh slumber; Welcome Oh pure light!"
Now the eye sees how to distinguish colors
It sees the difference between rubies and pebbles
The eye distinguishes jewels from dust
Hence, it is dust makes the eyes smart

> *He closes the book.*
> *He waits. They all ponder for a moment. Winter is not en-*
> *tirely sure what is going on. Maybe she surreptitiously checks*
> *the time on her phone.*
> *After a bit:*

is there anything you wanted to add, Carina?

CARINA
oh well
thank you Don

just briefly
I'll just say

thank you for the trust you're putting in me as we continue down
    this path

and I know
I know not everyone is continuing with us on this journey
and that's okay

because for the people in this room
and the people outside of this room for whom we're holding stake
it's really just a testament to how special a thing it is we have here

because it's a thing we Make Together

    Lights.

End of Play

NOTE ON CASTING WINTER

It is not necessary to cast a separate actor solely to play Winter, though you may certainly do so. The role was initially envisioned as a walk-on that could potentially be played by a different person every night. While this has been done successfully, most productions have opted instead to have the role played by an assistant stage manager or stagehand. This has the advantage of allowing you to rehearse and craft a final comic beat with that character.

NOTES ON PLAYING SCENE 3

1. It is *crucial* that the actors do not hold for laughs coming from the livestream comments. The scene is built to allow some of the lines to be lost.

2. The exception to this is Don, when he is responding directly to the comments. Starting on pg. 77, Don should read almost every comment in real time, so that he syncs up with the audience. The building anxiety he feels should mirror the chaos of the comments and audience reaction.

3. People read text at different speeds, so you need more than one comment visible at a time. The larger and more legible the font, the more funny the scene will be. Or conversely, the more effort the audience has to put into reading, the fewer laughs you will get.

4. Each livestream commenter should have a distinctive profile photo. This will help the audience to differentiate between the commenters, and heighten the irony as things go off the rails.

5. In a real livestream conversation, you would also have a live video feed of the people being recorded. Between the comments and the actors onstage there is already a large burden on the audience's attention. Adding a third element—a live video feed—will probably bring you diminishing returns.

6. In an actual live feed conversation, there would be many more floating emojis, "likes," etc. Adding more of these will dampen the comic effect and is not advisable.

ACKNOWLEDGMENTS

My gratitude to all the actors who supported the development of the play at Aurora: Elizabeth Carter, Kathryn Han, Denmo Ibrahim, Anna Ishida, Lance Gardner, John R. Lewis, Charisse Loriaux, Karen Offereins, Lisa Anne Porter, Rolf Saxon, Teddy Spencer, and Jomar Tagatac. Thanks to Tom Ross for taking a risk, to Adrienne Campbell-Holt for her indefatigable determination to bring the play to New York (newborn and all), to Kate Pines for changing everything, and especially to Josh Costello, for believing in the play when I did not.

Note on Songs/Recordings, Images, or Other Production Design Elements

Be advised that Broadway Licensing neither holds the rights to nor grants permission to use any songs, recordings, images, or other design elements mentioned in the play. It is the responsibility of the producing theater/organization to obtain permission of the copyright owner(s) for any such use. Aditional royalty fees may apply for the right to use copyrighted materials.

For any songs/recordings, images, or other design elements mentioned in the play, works in the public domain may be substituted. It is the producing theater/organization's responsibility to ensure the substituted work is indeed in the public domain. Broadway Licensing cannot advise as to whether or not a song/arrangement/recording, image, or other design element is in the public domain.

BV - #0013 - 260822 - C0 - 197/132/9 - PB - 9780822240570 - Matt Lamination